Contents

D0112712

Tay on the Trail

Written by Susan Bloom

Vowel Digraph *ai*

raining	trail	Gail
main	tail	plain
snail	wait	pain

Vowel Digraph *ay*

may	Tay	stray(ed)	stay
jay	way	gray	play

Inflected Ending *-ed*

asked	walked
barked	called
strayed	

High-Frequency Words

said	the	they
could	a	was
old	oh	what
you're	to	you'll

1

"It's not raining," said Dad.
"We can hike on the trail."
Gail asked, "May we take Tay?"

They walked on the trail.
Tay left the main path.
Gail could see his tail.

"Don't stray, Tay," called Gail.
Tay barked.
Did he spy a snake?

No, it was a plain old snail.
"Wait, Tay!" called Gail.
Tay didn't stay.
He barked more.

Did Tay spot a skunk?
No, it was a jay.
"This way, Tay!" called Gail.
Tay still strayed.

Tay barked more.
Oh, my! What was it?
It was a gray cat.

Gail said, "Tay, you're a pain.
The trail isn't a place to play.
Next time you'll stay home!"

My Family's Pets

Written by Helen Shay

Possessives

family's	Sam's	Dan's	pets'
cats'	Liz's	Brainy's	

Vowel Digraph *ay*

day　　　play　　　gray

Vowel Digraph *ai*

tail　　　Brainy　　　mailman

High-Frequency Words

do	many	are
of	have	from
you	a	
our	the	
to	and	

My family's pets do
many funny things.
Our pets' tales are lots of fun.

Have you ever seen a puppy sing?
Our big, black puppy Sam sings.
He can bark the notes and tap his tail.
Sam's songs go on and on.

11

Dan has twin cats.
Dan's cats run fast!
Muff and Puff zip
from place to place all day.

12

See the cats' bed.
Dan's cats like socks.
The cats play
with Dan's socks.

Liz's bird Brainy is big and gray.
Brainy likes to sit and talk.

Brainy likes the mailman.
Brainy tells him a silly joke.
Brainy's joke makes the mailman
smile.

15

Brainy's joke is funny.
Sam's songs are funny.
The cats are quick.
They are funny pets.

Jay's Ranch

Written by Dennis Burns

Vowel Digraphs *ai, ay*

Jay	rain	pail
waits	gray	day
stays		

Singular and Plural Possessives

Jay's	pail's	dog's
pigs'	horses'	

High-Frequency Words

worry	about	now
two	from	come
the	again	

17

Jay's ranch is hot.
It has not rained for days and days.
Jay must worry about his dog, horses,
and pigs.

If it rains, Jay will save rain.
Jay has a big pail that saves rain.
Jay's pail has pipes.

Jay waits and waits for rain.
Will it come on this gray day?
Yes, rain comes at last!
This rain stays for two days.

Rain fills Jay's big pail.
Now Jay can drain rain from the big
pail's pipes.

Jay fills his dog's pail.
Then he fills his pigs' pails.
Next Jay fills his horses' pails.

At last, it is Jay's turn.
Jay will not fill his pail yet.
That is not the main way Jay will use
his rain.

Jay enjoys his rain his way.
He plays in it and stays in it.
Then he will wait until it rains again.

Peaches and Cream

Written by Denise Ngo

Long e: Vowel Digraph ea

Bea	eats	meals	peas	peaches	gleam
Bea's	leaps	reach	dear	Dean	please
tea	Dean's	beak	sneaks	speaks	beats
heap	beams	feast	cream	real	treat

Short e: Vowel Digraph ea

bread	breath	meant	head

High-Frequency Words

lives	a	of
to	have	you
the	enough	are

25

Bea lives by a tree on a farm.
She eats meals of bread and peas.

In summer, ripe peaches gleam
on Bea's tree.
Bea takes a big breath and leaps up.
But she can't reach them.

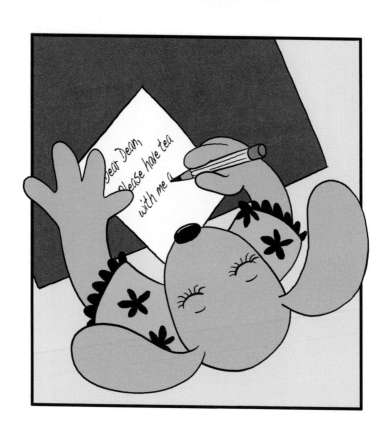

Bea sends a note to Dean.
"Dear Dean,
Please have tea with me
at my tree."

Bea asks, "Can you get the peaches?"
Is Dean's beak sharp enough?
No. The peaches must be meant to
stay on the tree.

Bea uses her head when Daisy
sneaks by.
Bea speaks to her.
"Can you get the peaches?"

Daisy gets up in the tree and
beats on the branch.
Peaches fall in a heap.
Bea beams.

Bea, Dean, and Daisy have
a feast.
Peaches and cream are
a real treat.

Bill Tried

Written by Julia Parrish

Adding Endings (Change *y* to *i*)

spied   flies
cried   tried

Possessives

Bill's   Fred's
Ann's

High-Frequency Words

what	do	old	friends
give	away	said	our
put	to	the	pushed
now			

Bill and his wife
cleaned Bill's shed.
What will Bill do
with his old things?

34

"We can give them away,"
said Bill.
"Our friends can take
all these things."

Fred rode by.
Fred spied Bill's funny fly.
"It still flies!" cried Fred.
Bill put Fred's fly on his cart.

Ann came.
Ann liked Bill's big rug.
She tried to jam it in her car.
Bill put Ann's rug by the fly.

Then Lee stopped.
Lee tried to lift Bill's trunk.
The trunk is as big as Lee!

Bill put the trunk on his cart.
Bill pushed the cart to each home.

Then Bill went home.
What will he put
in his shed now?

A Day at the Park

Written by Anita Flores

Adding Endings (Change *y* to *i*)

cried   tried   dried

Long *e*: Vowel Digraph *ea*

Jean   neat   treat   team   leaf   dream

Short *e*: Vowel Digraph *ea*

weather   wealth   instead

High-Frequency Words

to	the	was	said
enjoy	again	look	yellows
a	they	three	of
are			

Jean and Tom went to this park.
The weather was nice.
At the gate it said,
"Keep this park neat."

"We will treat it well
so that we can enjoy it again,"
Tom said.

"Look at this wealth of trees!"
Jean cried.
"These reds and yellows are
a nice treat."

Tom asked Jean,
"Can we play with that team?"
They played three games.

Then Tom sketched the sky on his art
pad.
Jean tried to sketch a dried leaf
instead.
She made it look nice.

46

At the lake, Jean and Tom
got to feed the ducks
and see big fish.

At last this fun day ended.
"Such a nice day!" Jean cried.
"It seemed like a dream."

Sloan's Goal

Written by Wallace Novak

Long o: Vowel Digraph oa

Sloan	floated	boats
soaked	coach	Joan
roamed	moaned	groaned
whoa	goal	

Long o: Vowel Digraph ow

Snow	grown	showed	blowing
growing	low	slow	flown
grow	row	crowed	

High-Frequency Words

the	a	enough
you	here	said
was	into	to
two		

Sloan and Snow floated boats
in the pond.
Snow got soaked.

A ball came by.
"May I play?" Sloan asked.
"You're not grown up enough,"
Dave claimed.

"I'm the coach," called Joan.
"Can you kick?"
Sloan showed her his best kick.
Joan said, "Play back here."

Sloan roamed back and forth.
The wind was blowing.
The grass was growing.
Snow moaned and groaned.

Just when Sloan was going,
the ball came at him. Whoa!
Sloan kicked it.

His kick was low and not slow.
Sloan pumped his arm. Yes!
The ball had flown into the goal.

"A goal!" yelled Dave.
"You don't need to grow!"
"I'll score two in a row,"
Sloan crowed.

Scram!

Written by Dante Pelayo

Three-Letter Consonant Blends

stream	shrubs	stripes	strong
string	splash	scream	scram

Consonant Pattern *-dge*

Madge	edge	budge

High-Frequency Words

a	saw	the
again	was	afraid
to	said	

Madge set up her tent.
She set up her tent by the edge
of a stream.
She made hot toast.

As she rested, Madge saw
a thing in the shrubs.
Then she saw it again.

It had stripes on its tail
and a dark mask.
It was as big as a cat.
Madge was not afraid.

She got a big, strong string.
She went to the stream
with the string.

"I will wait for that thing,"
Madge said.
"It will splash in this stream
and trip on my string."

Madge was brave and she
did not budge.
She did not scream.
That thing tripped on Madge's string.
"Scram!" yelled Madge.

The thing ran fast.
It did not stop.
Then Madge felt safe at camp.

Wait for Spring

Written by Renée McLean

Three-Letter Consonant Blends

scrap   sprang   sprinted   spring

Long *o*: Vowel Digraph *oa*

Toad   loaf   boat   coat

Long *o*: Vowel Digraph *ow*

pillow   showed   snow   row

Adding Endings (Change *y* to *i*)

cried   tried   dried

High-Frequency Words

saw   a   was   to
you   said   have   come
soon   the

Toad saw a scrap.
It was a map.
He made a plan.
"I must see Bird!" he cried.

Toad sprang up.
He tried to pack his pillow
and a hot loaf.

He sprinted to Bird's home.
"Bird!" he yelled.
"Can you read this map?"

Toad showed Bird the map.
"We must row in that boat.
We must follow this map.
We will be rich!"

"But, Toad," said Bird,
"I have jobs at home.
And snow may come soon."

Toad did not like snow.
"That is smart," said Toad.
"We will wait for spring."

Toad stuck the map in his coat.
He went to his snug home.
Then Toad dried his feet by the fire.

Just Right!

Written by Lynnette Rogers

Long *i*: Vowel Digraphs *ie, igh*

sight	tight	lie	high
might	light	night	right

Long *e*: Vowel Digraph *ie*

shriek   shield   field

High-Frequency Words

look	you	out
of	to	the
a	too	there

Let's play hide and seek.
Let me look for you.
I will shriek,
 "Hide out of sight!"

74

Try to hide in this box.
The lid will not close.
It is a tight fit.

Try to use that rug as a shield.
No, it is not big!
You are not out of sight!

Can you hide in this tree
in the field?
Sit on that branch.
No, it is too high.

Inside this cave might be fine.
No, there is no light.
It is dark like night!

By this shelf might be fine.
No, I can see you in the light!
Get out of sight!

Lie under this bed.
I will not see you.
Yes, this is just right!

Knots for Your Wrist

Written by Ben Hollis

Consonant Pattern _kn_

knots   knife   knows   knit

Consonant Pattern _wr_

wreath   wrist   wrote

Three-Letter Consonant Blends

string   strand   stripes

Long _i_: Vowel Digraphs _ie_, _igh_

light   pie   bright

High-Frequency Words

the   they   to   a
your   many   looks   put
what   with

Cam's class has
Arts and Crafts Day.
The kids bring things they made
to show the class.

Kay made a wreath with her mom
to hang on her wall.
Her wreath is light green and pink.
It smells sweet.

Len uses string for your wrist.
He ties many knots.
He gave a short strand
to each kid in class.

84

Jill baked pumpkin pie muffins.
She baked with her dad.
Her dad has a knife to
cut the muffins.

Jane wrote a skit.
She shows her skit
while the class looks on.
Her skit is funny.

Don painted a ship.
His art looks real.
Don's mom put
it in a frame.

What did Cam bring?
Cam knows how to knit!
He has a bright
scarf with stripes that he made.

Barb Knows!

Written by Kiran Smedley

Consonant Pattern *kn*

knife   knows

Consonant Pattern *wr*

wrote

Long *i*: Vowel Digraphs *ie, igh*

pie   high   right

Long *e*: Vowel Digraph *ie*

brief   niece   believes

Comparative Endings -er, -est

freshest   sharper   highest

High-Frequency Words

said   of   to
the   how   was

"I will make my pie,"
said Barb.
She wrote a brief list
of things to use.

Barb got the freshest peaches.
She cut the peaches
with a sharper knife.

Barb asked her niece to get nice
plums.
"I will add them
to my pie."

Barb's niece and her pal
gave plums for the pie.
Barb's pie got bigger.

Barb believes she knows how to
make her pie big.
She piles more peaches and plums
on top of her pie.

Barb's pie was high.
"It's not quite as high as the
sky yet,"
Barb said with a smile.

Barb put nuts right on top.
"That is how I like my pie,"
Barb said.
"It is the highest pie!"

Seaside Daydreams

Written by Joel Dorsch

Compound Words

seashore	lunchtime	daydream(s)	baseball
teammates	homemade	treetops	backstage
showtime	sailboat	starfish	stingrays
spaceship	sunset	seaside	

Long e: Vowel Digraph ea

seashore	meal	daydream
teammates	seaside	

Short e: Vowel Digraph ea

head	breath	meant

High-Frequency Words

a	are	the
they	to	above
their		

97

Five kids and a mom are spending
a happy day at the seashore.
After a lunchtime meal they rest in the
shade and daydream.

Carl dreams in his head, "I'm pitching
in a baseball game.
My teammates and I are winning
10–0!"

Eve dreams, "I'm flying
in my own homemade plane.
It skims above the treetops."

Rick dreams, "I'm backstage
waiting for my turn to go on.
I take a deep breath and it's
showtime!"

Libby dreams, "I'm drifting
on a sailboat.
I can see starfish and stingrays!"

Ray dreams, "I'm on a spaceship
meant to go to Mars.
I hope I don't get lost!"

At sunset Mom tells the kids,
"It's time to go home."
But the kids will keep
their seaside daydreams.

Clues for Sue

Written by Jacob Payton

Vowel Digraphs *ue, ew, ui*

Sue	few	clue(s)
fruit	new	blue
suit	chew	knew

Consonant Pattern *kn*

knows knitted knots

Consonant Pattern *wr*

wrote wreath

Long *o:* Vowel Digraph *oa*

goal coat roam

Long *o:* Vowel Digraph *ow*

knows show grow

High-Frequency Words

a	the	to	look
of	find	said	touch
laughs	was	were	around

105

Dad knows a game for Sue.
The goal is to find a few clues that
Dad wrote.

Dad shows Sue her first clue.
"The first clue is by that fruit,"
said Dad.
"It is in that bright blue pot."

Sue reads her first clue.
"Take six steps to Dad's desk.
Touch the pad to see the next clue."

Sue reads her new clue.
"Look for the trail up the steps."
Sue runs to the steps.

She laughs.
The trail is made of Dad's knitted
socks.
Sue spots the clue by Dad's bed.
"Find Dad's new blue coat."

110

Sue reads her last clue.
"He likes to bark, run, roam,
and chew on knots. He will grow
big!"

Dad hugged Sue.
"I knew this pup was right for Sue."
Sue's arms were like a wreath around
that pup!

The Blue Crew

Written by Wes Long

Vowel Digraphs *ew, ue, ui*

Blue   Crew   cruise
flew   newsstand

Long *e*: Vowel Digraph *ie*

Chiefs   shriek   field

High-Frequency Words

a   the   again
where   above   paper
they   are

113

This is a big baseball game
for the Blue Crew. They play the
Green Chiefs.
Will the team be the champs?

114

It is Zack's last turn at bat.
He swings. He misses.
He swings again. He misses.

Will Zack get a hit?
Will Zack cruise the bases?
He grips his bat.
Zack swings hard. Crack!

116

Dads and moms jump up and shriek!
Where did that ball go?

That ball is not
inside the field.
That ball flew
above tall trees!

118

That is Zack's first hit!
The Blue Crew wins.
They are the champs!

Zack stops at the newsstand
the next day.
His snapshot is in the paper.
Zack is a baseball star!

Helpful Advice

Written by Laura Zuccari

Suffixes *-ly, -ful*

deeply	helpful	frightful	clearly	fearful
plainly	wildly	painful	sadly	wisely
hopeful	graceful	hardly	grateful	

Vowel Digraphs *ue, ew, ui*

Prue	blue	cruised	Newt
few	new	suit	

High-Frequency Words

what	do	was	a
said	were	to	the
would	wanted		

Prue sighed deeply.
"What can I do?"
Mom was helpful.
"Take a class," she said.

Prue tried an art class.
Her paintings were all blue and
frightful.
Clearly, art was not for Prue.

Prue tried an acting class.
When she got on stage,
she felt fearful.
Plainly, acting was not for Prue.

124

Prue tried to ride a horse.
The horse cruised wildly, and
the ride was painful.
Sadly, horses were not for Prue.

Mom wisely chose Prue's next class.
Would Prue like it?
Mom and Prue felt hopeful.

Coach Newt showed Prue a dive.
Prue's dive was graceful.
It hardly made a splash.
Prue wanted to do a few more
dives in her new suit.

Hurray! Dives were for Prue.
Prue and Mom felt grateful.

Zoom! Zoom!

Written by Rob Stern

Vowel Sound in *moon: oo*

zoo	zoomed	coo
noon	food	hoops
too		

High-Frequency Words

many	to	the
other	they	were
thought	was	what
you	do	remember

129

Luke is fast.
He walks so fast
that he misses
many things.

130

Luke went to the zoo.
Luke went past apes.
Other kids stopped.
Luke zoomed on.

Luke sped past snakes.
They were huge!
Other kids stayed to look.
Luke zoomed on.

Luke zipped past birds.
"Coo, coo," called bright birds.
Luke did not stop.
He zoomed on.

At noon a man
gave food to the fish.
Fish swim fast for food!
Luke zoomed on.

134

Seals threw balls in hoops.
All the kids thought it was fun.
Luke missed the show.

"What did you see at the zoo?"
Mom asked.
"I do not remember!" cried Luke.
"It all went by too fast!"

To the Moon

Written by Reonne Reed

Vowel Sound in *moon: oo*

moon	tools	food
too	room	

Suffixes *-ly, -ful*

quickly	safely
hopeful	sadly

High-Frequency Words

a	they	to
the	there	said
water	oh	again

Kim and Dan made a plan.
They will go up to the Moon!

"Can we get there?" Kim asked.
"We will need a big spaceship."

Dan quickly got tools.
"Use those tools safely,"
he said.

When they made the ship,
Kim got food for them.
"Is this all we need?" she asked.

"We need water too," Dan said.
He filled his jug.
He got a jug for Kim too.

Kim and Dan got in.
It had lots of room.
Dan was hopeful.

The big spaceship did not start.
"Oh, well," Dan said sadly.
"We can try again."

Browny the Clown

Written by Flora Foss

Diphthong *ow*

Browny	gown	clown(s)	town	cows	owls
wow	crowd	now	how	growls	down
pow	howl	crowd	bow	frowning	

Diphthong *ou*

around	couch	Bouncy	out	loud	mouth

Vowel Sound in *moon: oo*

boots	balloons	tools	room	too

High-Frequency Words

puts	a	the	into
find	looks	are	people
two			

145

Browny puts on a red nose and wig.
She puts on a silly gown and
huge boots. Why?
Browny is a clown.

146

Browny is the best clown around
town.
She uses balloons as tools and makes
them into cows or owls.
Her dances will make you say, "Wow!"

A crowd is waiting, but
Browny is frowning. Why?
Clowns need painted faces.
Browny can't find her paints.

148

Browny looks in each box and
under the couch.
She looks all around the room.
Maybe Bouncy the dog can help.
But how?

Bouncy barks and growls out loud.
Browny cries, "Not now, Bouncy!"
Bouncy leaps at the shelf.
Down falls a case! Pow!

150

Browny's paints are in the case.
Her mouth now has a smile.
"Thanks, Bouncy!"

People howl at Browny.
The people howl at Bouncy too.
The crowd claps, and two clowns bow.

A Bundle of Shirts

Written by Eric Weiss

Final Syllable -le

| little | simple | bundle | sample | dimple |

Diphthong ow

| town | brown | frown | flowers |

Diphthong ou

| house | mouth | out |

High-Frequency Words

school	was	a
they	the	wanted
of	to	one

Jen will start school soon.
She needs new stuff.
She was happy.
So was her mom.

Jen tried on a brown shirt.
It was too little.
Jen tried on a red shirt.
It was too big.

Jen's mom planned on
getting a shirt for Jen.
They left the house to go shoppi
at the mall in town.

Jen's mom planned on
getting a shirt for Jen.
They left the house to go shopping
at the mall in town.

Jen tried on a brown shirt.
It was too little.
Jen tried on a red shirt.
It was too big.

Jen tried on a simple blue shirt.
It had a big rip.
She did not see
a shirt she wanted.
Her mouth was in a frown.

157

Her mom asked the clerk
if he had a cute shirt for Jen.
He got out a bundle of
shirts to sample.
One shirt had flowers on it.

A green shirt in the bundle
fit Jen nicely.
It was not too little or too big.

Jen's smile was so big
that her dimple showed.
She gave her mom a big hug.

Don't Stumble

Written by Stacey Adams

Final Syllable -*le*

gobble   little   stumble

Diphthong *ow*

wow   town   down   brown

Diphthong *ou*

cloud   ground   bounds

High-Frequency Words

of	to	the
do	a	everyone
there	remembers	what
said	great	here

This is Sam's big day.
No cloud is in the sky.
He jumps out of his bed.

Sam has on his brown pants.
He runs down to eat.
He tries to gobble down his food.
He cannot sit still.

He and his mom and dad
go to the track.
Mom and Dad tell him
to do his best.

Now a big crowd is here.
Everyone in this little town
might be here!
Wow!

Sam gets in line on the ground.
He sees the tape far away.
He must get there first.

Sam bounds down the lane.
He is fast.
He remembers what
Mom and Dad said.

How fast Sam runs!
He must not stumble.
Sam is first!
This is a great day for Sam.

168

Puppy Roundup

Written by Aiko Ozu

Vowel Patterns *ow, ou*

count	doghouse	found	brown	grow
mound	Cloud	bounces	slow	bow
mouth	grouchy	sour	low	wow
loudly	shout	ouch	shows	
sound	our	Scout	bowl	
mouse	pounces	crouches	couch	
roundup	snouts	hounds		

Final Syllable *-le*

little   gobble   able   circle

High-Frequency Words

the	one	looks	a
ears	never	others	people
behind	into		

Count the brown puppies in the
doghouse.
I found one brown puppy in that
mound.
I found five puppies in all.
Now let's meet each puppy up
close.

170

Cloud is peppy and happy.
She bounces when she walks, and
her mouth looks like a smile.

Pickle is a little grouchy and a little slow.
Did he just gobble a sour ball?
Or maybe he needs a nice nap.

172

Bow Wow is able to bark loudly.
Please do not shout, Bow Wow.
Ouch! That sound hurts our ears.

Scout never barks at all.
She is like a mouse.
She crouches low and sneaks up on
the others.
Then she pounces!

174

Moon is shy around new people.
He crouches behind the couch.
Then when it seems safe,
he shows his face.

Drew calls, "Dinnertime!"
It's a puppy roundup.
Five snouts circle the bowl.
Soon the puppies will grow
into big hounds.

Begin to Dance

Written by Jamey Ryndak

177

Pam will start dance class.
Pam is afraid.
Will she be left out?

"What a sour face!" said Mom.
"Did you eat a lemon?
Smile! It will be fun."
Mom pats Pam's cheek.

179

Pam will try to dance.
Pam will step with her feet.
She will swing her
arms behind her.

Pam will bring her hands high
and open them.
All of the girls do the same.

Class ends so fast!
Pam opens her mouth.
She begins to smile.
She is happy.

Pam can dance now!
She will not frown and look sour.
Her feet are happy at class!
Pam likes to dance.

Pam shows that she can dance all
day.
She bends, turns, spins, and glides.
At home there is no limit.

184

Time for Bed

Written by Leslie Lin

Syllables V/CV, VC/V

silent	opened	began	never

Vowel Patterns *ow, ou*

brow	mouth	count	found	down
low	couch	howl	loud	growing
know	frowned	drowsy		

High-Frequency Words

what	was	to
said	behind	

185

"What time is it?"
asked Mom.
Ted's brow went up but he was
silent.

186

"Is it time to eat?" asked Ted.
Ted opened his mouth.
"No, it's not time to eat,"
said Mom.

"Is it time to count?"
asked Ted.
"No, it's not time to count,"
said Mom.

"Is it time to hide
and be found?" asked Ted.
Ted hid down low behind the couch.
"No, it's not time to hide," said Mom.

189

"Is it time to howl?" asked Ted.
Ted began to be loud.
"No, it's never time to howl,"
said Mom.

190

Ted was growing sleepy.
"I know it's time for bed," he said.
Mom nodded.
Ted frowned.

Ted's lids became drowsy.
"It's time to close my eyes,"
said Ted.
He went to sleep.

The Rooks' Farm

Written by Felix Hechter

Miss Hood took us to the Rooks'
farm.
"Look at how the Rooks live,"
she told us.
"Then write in your open
notebooks."

Woof! Woof! The dog didn't
know us.
He begins to let the Rooks know
we had come.

First, we looked inside the cabin.
Food cooked in pots hung on hooks
over a wood fire.

Jenny Rook spun yarn
from sheep's wool.
She will use the yarn to knit a
hooded blanket for the new baby.

197

Simon and Becky Rook dipped
pails in the brook.
It took them seven trips
to get enough water for one day!

Dan Rook showed us how
he cleans a horse's hoof.
That's its foot.
That horse just about stood on *my*
foot!

Soon we had to say good-bye.
The Rooks shook hands with us.
We had a good time
at the Rooks' farm.

Hiking and Racing

Written by Drew Copperfield

Adding Endings (Drop Final e)

named   liked   smiled
hiking   raced

Vowel Sound in *foot: oo*

woods   cook   looked
book   good

Plurals *-es*

bushes
foxes
lunches

High-Frequency Words

family   to   the   a
very   were   colors   said
could   saw   are   our
was

201

My family camps out.
We go to the woods.
We cook outside
and sleep in tents.

Last time we went,
we left at sunrise.
Dad, Mom, Ben, Jake, and I
got in our car.
I slept all the way.

The woods are in a park.
That park is named
Grand Lake State Park.
I liked it very much.

204

The leaves on the trees and bushes
were nice colors.
The lake looked fine
in the sunshine.
We all smiled.

A map in our book
showed walking paths.
We went hiking and saw baby foxes!
Dad set up our tents
and made good lunches.

206

We raced to the big lake.
Mom said we could
go fishing the next day.
We got a huge fish!

Our camping trip
was fun.
We cannot wait
for our next camping trip.

208

Racing to Clean

Written by Sarah Park

Adding Endings (Drop Final e)

raced	joked	hiding
liked	racing	smiling

Vowel Sound in *foot: oo*

looked	good
books	took

High-Frequency Words

to	said	a	they
about	was	you	

209

Emmy went to see Danny.
Danny looked sad.
"I cannot play,"
Danny said sadly.

"My chores are not finished."
"We can still play," Emmy said.

"We can make cleaning a game!
This is a good starting place."
Emmy and Danny
raced to pick things up.

212

They joked about
Danny's messy ways.
Cleaning was fun
and not dull.

213

Emmy found lost books
hiding in Danny's big trunk.
Danny found a hat he liked.
He found racing cars with his blocks.

214

Danny's mom took a look.
"Good job!" she said.
"We played all day!"
Emmy said, smiling.

"Can you play a cleaning
game next week?"
Danny asked.

Roy and Joyce Join In

Written by Regina Belasco

Pride and Joy

Diphthongs *oi, oy*

Floyd	Joy	Hoy	boy	join	Roy	Joyce
oils	joints	coils	hoist	voice	choice	toy
boil	noisy	moist	spoil	joyful	soil	

Inflected Ending *-es*

rushes   crashes   watches

Adding Endings (Drop Final *e*)

named   smiling   races

High-Frequency Words

a	the	across
into	they	have
everything	again	are

Floyd owns a sailboat
named Pride and Joy.
In the summer Floyd sails his boat
across huge Lake Hoy.

218

This time a boy and a girl join
the sailboat's crew.
Roy and Joyce will help Floyd.
They are smiling.

Roy oils gears and joints.
Joyce wraps ropes into neat coils.
They help hoist the sails.

The crew races quickly when
Floyd talks.
They have no choice.
Floyd is in charge.

The sailboat rushes into a bad storm.
It bounces like a toy boat in a bathtub.
A wave boils up and crashes on
deck.

At last, the noisy wind and rain
die down.
Floyd watches the sky.
He says, "It's clearing up."

Everything is a little moist,
but a storm can't spoil this trip.
Still, the crew is joyful when
they step on soil again.

224

Teacher, Actor, or Sailor

Written by Grace Hammond

Decodable Practice Reader 28B

Suffixes -er, -or

teacher   actor   sailor
singer   doctor

Diphthongs oi, oy

boys   choice   Joy   hoist
voice   joyful   join

High-Frequency Words

what   you   become
anything   they   a
school   work   people
your   the

What will you be
when you grow up?
Boys and girls can become anything
if they try hard.

226

Pete's choice is a teacher.
He will teach reading and writing.
Pete likes school.
He is smart.

Joy will be an actor.
She will act on stage.
Joy is funny.
She is not shy.

228

Tom will be a sailor.
He will work on a ship.
Tom will hoist sails.
He likes feeling the wind on his face.

Dan will be a singer.
He will sing songs.
Dan has a nice voice.
Being on stage makes him joyful.

230

Kim will be a doctor.
She will help people.
She will work hard.

What is your dream?
Join in!
You can be a teacher, an actor,
a sailor—or anything!

232

A Writer and an Actor

Written by Howard Price

Suffixes -er, -or

writer	actor
baker	farmer

Diphthongs *oi, oy*

joy	toys
boys	moist
choice	soil

High-Frequency Words

a	family	who
the	of	to
are	they	

Sue must make
a family tree.
A family tree shows
who is in her family.
234

Sue starts with her mom.
Mom is a writer.
She writes books.
Sue likes her mom's books.

Sue's dad is an actor.
He acts with much joy.
Sue's dad is a good actor.

Mom's dad made all sorts of toys.
Mom's mom ran a toy shop.
Girls and boys liked
to see those nice toys.

Dad's mom is a baker.
She makes buns.
They are always moist.

Dad's dad made the choice to be a
farmer.
He made things grow
in rich, brown soil.

Sue made her family tree.
She showed all these facts.
Sue is proud of her family!

It Is No One's Fault !

Written by Sam Kowalski

Vowel Sound in *ball: aw, au*

Dawn	Paul	coleslaw
flaws	thawed	because
sauce	hauls	raw
straw(s)	pause	bawls
fault	squawks	crawls
sprawls	draw	

High-Frequency Words

are	their	a
the	of	to
who	they	

Dawn and Paul are fixing
meat loaf and coleslaw for dinner.
Their plan has a few flaws.

242

First, the meat is not thawed. Why?
Because Dawn left it in the freezer.
Next, the sauce burns in its pot. Why?
Because Paul didn't stir it
on the stove.

When Dawn hauls the meat loaf
out of the oven, it is raw inside.
Why? Because Paul didn't turn on
the oven.

The coleslaw tastes like straw.
Why? Because Dawn didn't pause
to add oil or spices.

245

Paul bawls at Dawn, "This isn't
my fault!"
Dawn squawks back, "This isn't
my fault!"

246

Dawn crawls on the couch.
Paul sprawls on the rug.
The meal was not Dawn's fault.
It was not Paul's fault.
They need to think for a time.

Later, Paul and Dawn draw straws
to see who will clean up the mess.

Oatmeal!

Written by Leona Burns

Decodable Practice Reader

29B

Syllable Patterns: Vowel Digraphs and Diphthongs

oatmeal	boyhood	cowboy
cookouts	soybean	seaweed
football		

High-Frequency Words

early	one	to	a
said	learn	school	science
was	through	could	I
are	of		

Early one morning, Carla
ate oatmeal.
She asked Dad why he did not.
"I used to eat a lot of it," Dad said.

"It started in my boyhood.
I liked a show about a cowboy.
That cowboy ate oatmeal, so I ate
oatmeal."

"I had oatmeal for breakfast.
At times, I had it for lunch and
supper. I really liked it."

"Later at scout cookouts, I had to
learn to make oatmeal.
I made raisin oatmeal, banana
oatmeal, and plum oatmeal."

"In high school, I even did a science project about oatmeal. I made soybean and seaweed oatmeal snacks!"

"All I could think about was oatmeal. I even had daydreams about it running over football fields and through malls!"

"I get it," said Carla.
"Now you are sick of oatmeal!"
Dad grinned and said, "A little."

The Ball

Written by Lincoln Burns

It was a windy August day.
It felt like fall, not summer.
Kids, moms, and dads still
played baseball.

The field was in an old park.
An oatmeal factory was
on one side.
An old soybean oil factory was
next to it.

Early in the game, Paul's dad came
to bat.
Dad was big.
In his boyhood, Dad was a football
player.

Paul yelled, "This wind will carry a ball far.
If you hit the ball hard, it will fly over the outfield fence, Dad."

Dad looked at the fence.
Behind it, Dad saw the river.
Dad said, "I will not try to hit the
ball that far, Paul."

Paul asked, "Why not?"
"The ball might fall in the river,"
answered Dad.
"Yes, and be a home run!"
said Paul.

"But this game will end,"
explained Dad.
"Why?" asked Paul.
Dad grinned, rubbed his
jaw, and said, "Because we
have just one ball."

Untie and Rewrap

Written by Isabelle Giroux

Prefixes un-, re-

relight	unwraps	rewrap	replay
unwise	unhappy	unending	reties
untie	rereads		

Vowel Sound in ball: aw, au

Saul	bawls	pause
because	crawls	

High-Frequency Words

today	a	the
to	again	of
wants	many	four
too	are	

265

Saul is four today.
Mom and Dad throw a party
for him and three pals.

Saul blows out the candles.
He likes that, so he asks Mom
to relight them.
Saul blows out the candles again.

Saul unwraps all of his gifts.
He likes that too, so he starts
to rewrap the gifts.
He wants to unwrap them again.

Saul and his pals play Pin the Tail
on the Dog.
Saul makes them replay the game
again and again.

Dad tells Saul, "No more repeating."
That's unwise.
It makes Saul unhappy, and
he bawls and bawls.
His cries are unending.

270

So Dad reties ribbons on boxes.
Saul can untie them many times.
Mom reads cards to Saul.
She rereads them many times.

Mom and Dad can now pause
because this day is over.
Even Saul crawls up for a nap!

272

Old Jo

Written by Trevor Stanton

Long *o: o*

post	old	most
gold	hold	told
cold		

Long *i: i*

| unwinds | mild | wild |

High-Frequency Words

the	of	a
loves	color	together
to	does	you

At the end of this road,
at the top of a post,
is the home of Old Jo
and the things he loves most.

His nest made of straw
is the color of gold,
and he fills it with
all the food it can hold.

Old Jo grabs a twig
and unwinds a string,
and he ties them together
to make a nice swing.

276

He sings and caws
with his voice that is mild.
Then he flies in the sky
on a ride that is wild.

Old Jo has a coat
that is black, I am told.
He crows all day long—
on hot days or cold.

278

He does not undress
when he's ready for bed.
He just fluffs up his coat
and tucks down his head.

279

When you think of Old Jo—
his nest, swing, and all—
Think of the fun things
that you can recall.

Three Kind Birds

Written by Jane Marks

Long *o*: *o*

old
cold

Long *i*: *i*

find
kind
mind

High-Frequency Words

a	the	to
of	water	you
said	do	have

Dee is a small bird.
She plays in the woods.
She went to different parts
of the woods. She got lost.

Dee felt unhappy.
She had no water.
She did not have much food.
Dee sat down and cried.

Three birds came.
"Did you get lost?"
asked the one old bird.

"Yes," she said.
"I am lost,
and my bottle is dry."

The birds took Dee
to a cold stream.
The birds refilled her bottle
and gave her bread.

286

Those birds helped Dee
find her way home.
"You are kind," said Dee's mom.

The three birds smiled.
"We are kind.
We do not mind."

Grade **1.3**

Scott Foresman

Decodable
Practice Readers
19A-30C
Volume 3
Units 4 and 5

Scott Foresman
is an imprint of

Glenview, Illinois • Boston, Massachusetts • Chandler, Arizona
• Upper Saddle River, New Jersey

ISBN-13: 978-0-328-49216-9
ISBN-10:   0-328-49216-7
11 V011 14 13
CC1